Earth's Mountains

Bobbie Kalman

Crabtree Publishing Company

www.crabtreebooks.com

Created by Bobbie Kalman

For Ron Bator, a long-lost friend and brother in spirit
I wrote this book during your time in Nepal.
Our conversation inspired me to great heights!

Author and Editor-in-Chief
Bobbie Kalman

Research
Robin Johnson

Editor
Kathy Middleton

Proofreader
Crystal Sikkens

Design
Bobbie Kalman
Katherine Berti
Samantha Crabtree (cover)

Production coordinator
Katherine Berti

Prepress technician
Margaret Amy Salter

Consultant
Joel Mercer,
former Head of the Geography Department,
Galt Collegiate Institute

Illustrations
Barbara Bedell: pages 24 (leaves), 25 (lichens)
Katherine Berti: pages 12, 24-25 (background)
Robert MacGregor: page 10 (top)
Margaret Amy Salter: pages 11, 14, 17, 18

Photographs
© Dreamstime.com: page 18
© iStockphoto.com: pages 20, 23 (top)
Property of Bobbie Kalman: page 30 (inset)
© Shutterstock.com: front and back cover, pages 3, 4, 5, 6, 7 (bottom), 8, 9, 10 (bottom), 11, 13, 14, 15, 16, 17, 19, 21, 22, 23 (middle and bottom), 24, 25, 26, 27 (except inset), 28, 29, 30 (except inset), 31
Other images by Corbis, Digital Stock, and Photodisc

Library and Archives Canada Cataloguing in Publication

Kalman, Bobbie, 1947-
Earth's mountains / Bobbie Kalman.

(Looking at earth)
Includes index.
ISBN 978-0-7787-3207-5 (bound).--ISBN 978-0-7787-3217-4 (pbk.)

1. Mountains--Juvenile literature. I. Title. II. Series.

GB512.K34 2008 j551.43'2 C2008-905558-6

Library of Congress Cataloging-in-Publication Data

Kalman, Bobbie.
Earth's mountains / Bobbie Kalman.
p. cm. -- (Looking at Earth)
Includes index.
ISBN-13: 978-0-7787-3217-4 (pbk. : alk. paper)
ISBN-10: 0-7787-3217-7 (pbk. : alk. paper)
ISBN-13: 978-0-7787-3207-5 (reinforced library binding : alk. paper)
ISBN-10: 0-7787-3207-X (reinforced library binding : alk. paper)
1. Mountains--Juvenile literature. I. Title.
GB512.K35 2009
551.43'2--dc22
2008036594

Crabtree Publishing Company

Printed in the U.S.A./102016/CG20160822

www.crabtreebooks.com 1-800-387-7650
 In Canada: We acknowledge the financial support of the Government of Canada through the Canada Book Fund for our publishing activities.

Published in Canada
Crabtree Publishing
616 Welland Ave.
St. Catharines, ON
L2M 5V6

Published in the United States
Crabtree Publishing
PMB 59051
350 Fifth Avenue, 59th Floor
New York, New York 10118

Published in the United Kingdom
Crabtree Publishing
Maritime House
Basin Road North, Hove
BN41 1WR

Published in Australia
Crabtree Publishing
3 Charles Street
Coburg North
VIC, 3058

Contents

What are mountains? 4
Mountains on Earth 6
Mountain ranges 8
Made of rock 10
Earth's plates 12
Fold mountains 14
Faults and blocks 16
Dome mountains 18
Volcanic mountains 20
Changing mountains 22
Mountain plants 24
Mountain animals 26
Living on mountains 28
Mountains of fun! 30
Words to know and Index 32

What are mountains?

Mountains are areas of rocky land that rise high above the ground. They are big, tall, **landforms**. Landforms are different shapes of land on Earth. Most mountains have **steep** sides. Steep sides rise almost straight up from the ground. They make mountains hard to climb!

What are hills?

Hills are short, small mountains with **sloping** sides. Sloping sides are not very steep. Hills are much easier to climb than mountains are!

*The **peak** of a mountain is narrow and pointed. A mountain's sides are steep. Its **base**, or bottom, is wide.*

Mountains on Earth

Mountains cover almost one-quarter of the Earth's **surface**. They are on every **continent** in the world. Continents are seven huge land areas on Earth. Mountains are also found in **oceans**. Oceans are big bodies of salty water. This mountain is located in the Southern Ocean in Antarctica.

Sizes and shapes

Mountains are different sizes and shapes. Some tall mountains reach high up into the clouds. Other mountains are shorter and wider. Some mountains have rough, jagged peaks. Others have flat or rounded **summits**. A summit is the highest place on a mountain.

This mountain peak reaches above the clouds.

Mount Kilimanjaro is the highest mountain in Africa. Its summit is rounded.

Mountain ranges

Most mountains are part of **mountain ranges**. Mountain ranges are groups of mountains that are close together. There are many mountain ranges on Earth. The Himalayas in Asia are Earth's highest mountain range. The Andes in South America form the world's longest mountain range. The Rocky Mountains, or Rockies, in North America, make up the second-longest range. They run from northwestern Canada to the southwestern United States.

The Himalayas stretch across six countries in Asia and have the highest peaks in the world, including Mount Everest. Mount Everest is the highest mountain on Earth.

The Andes form the longest mountain range. This guanaco lives high on a mountain that is part of the Andes.

These skiers are at the top of one of the Rocky Mountains in Canada.

The Alps are a range of mountains in Europe. The Matterhorn is part of the Alps. It has a tall, sharp peak.

Made of rock

Mountains are made of rock. They are part of Earth's **crust**. The crust is the rocky top layer of Earth. We live on Earth's crust. Under the crust, there is a layer of Earth called the **mantle**. The mantle contains **magma**. Magma is red-hot melted rock. Much of Earth's crust is covered by plants, water, and buildings, but you can see the crust on rocky mountains.

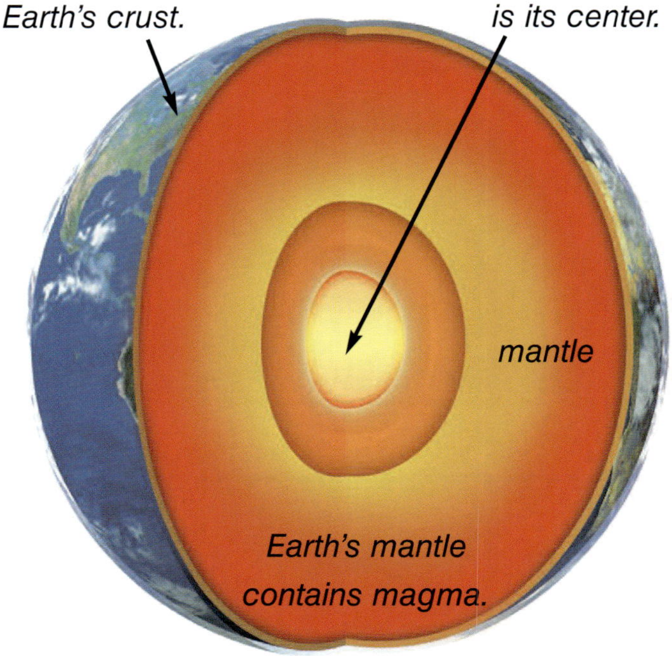

You can see Earth's crust on this mountain.

Many kinds of plants cover Earth's crust.

Rock groups

Earth's crust is made up of three main types of rocks, which form in different ways. **Igneous**, or fiery, rocks form when magma cools and hardens. **Sedimentary** rocks form when tiny pieces of clay and sand build up in layers and form new rock. **Metamorphic** rocks are rocks that change when they are heated and pressed into shape deep inside Earth.

*The Taj Mahal in India is made of white **marble**. Marble is a metamorphic rock. It is a changed form of limestone.*

*This **granite** has a frog shape.*

Granite is an igneous rock that forms from magma under the ground.

*These rocks are **basalt**. They came from a **volcano**.*

*Basalt is an igneous rock that forms from cooled **lava**.*

*This **limestone** is inside a cave.*

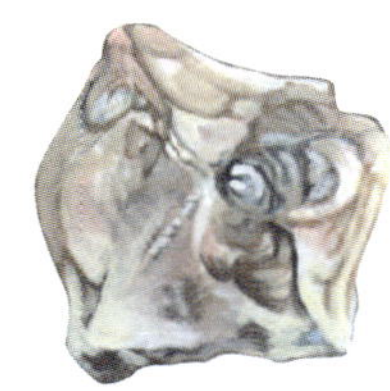

Limestone is a sedimentary rock that forms inside caves.

*This **sandstone** rock looks like a tree.*

Sandstone is a sedimentary rock made mainly of sand.

Earth's plates

Earth's crust is made up of **tectonic plates**. Tectonic plates are huge pieces of rock that fit together like a giant puzzle. There are seven very large plates on Earth. They are shown on this map. There are also many smaller plates. The tectonic plates sit on hot liquid magma. Liquid magma causes Earth's plates to move very slowly. Some plates move toward one another, and others move apart. The arrows show in which direction the plates are moving. Over time, the movements of some plates create mountains.

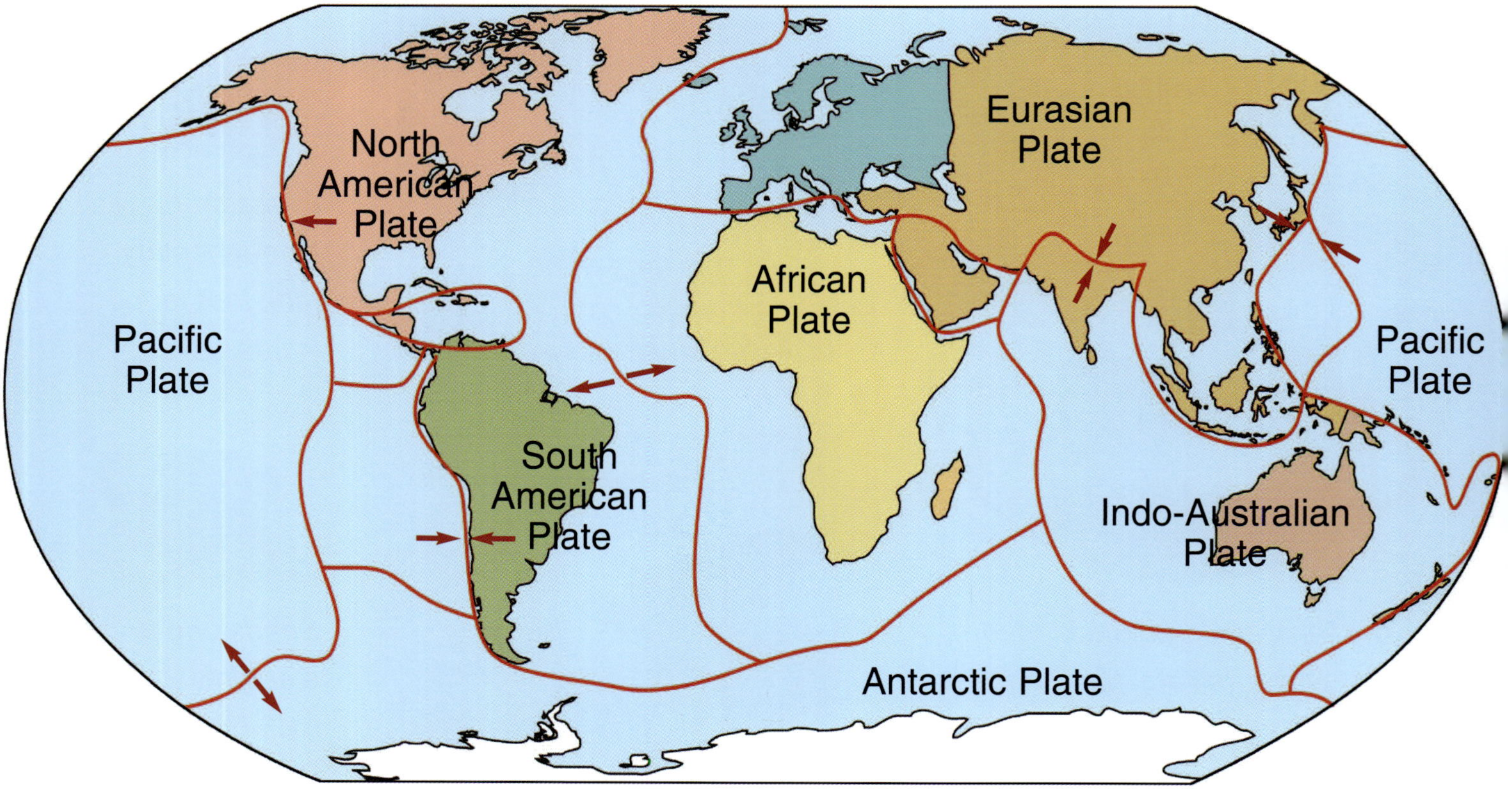

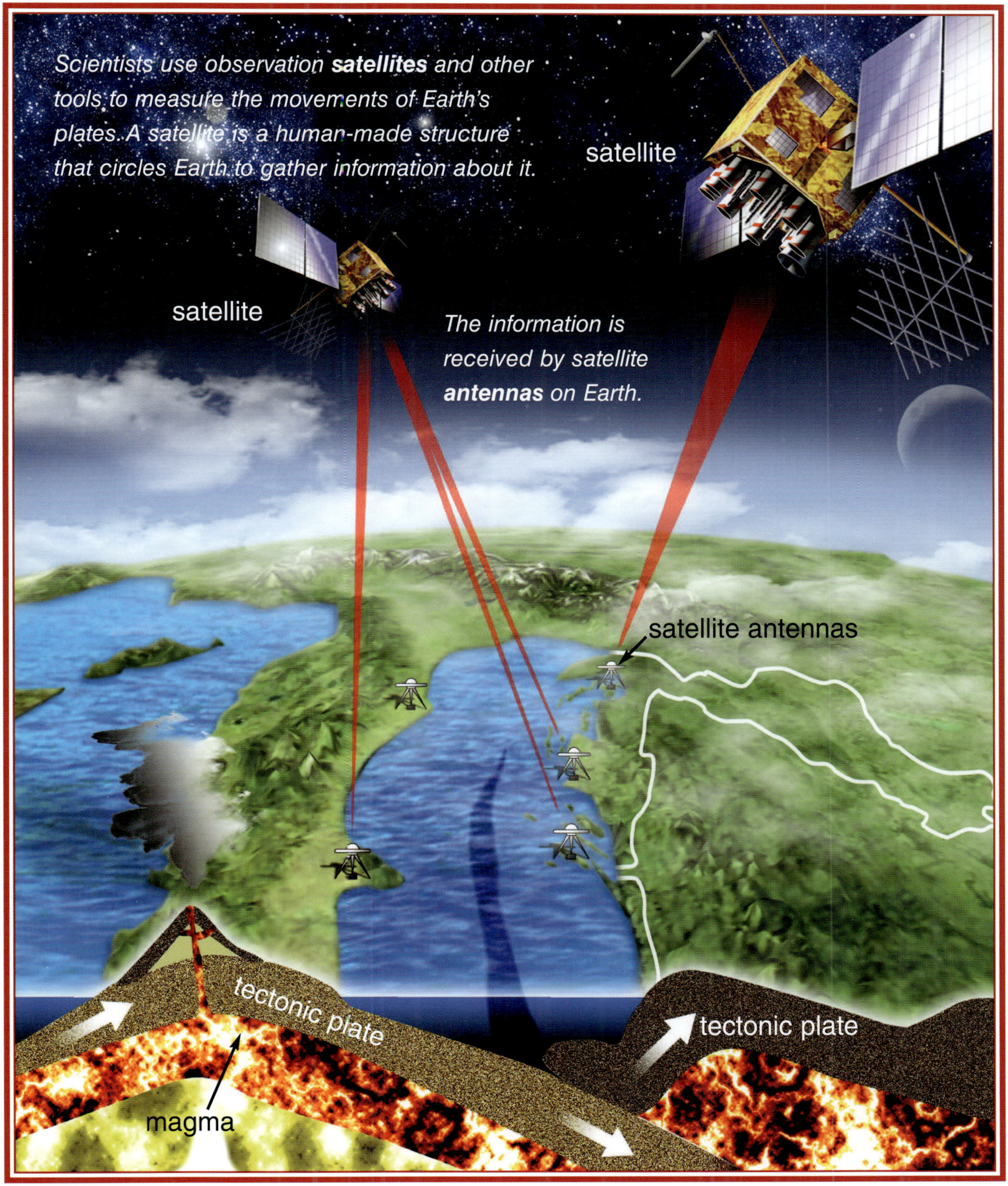
Scientists use observation **satellites** and other tools to measure the movements of Earth's plates. A satellite is a human-made structure that circles Earth to gather information about it.
satellite
satellite
The information is received by satellite **antennas** on Earth.
satellite antennas
tectonic plate
tectonic plate
magma

Fold mountains

Earth's plates are made up of layers of rock. The layers of rock are called **strata**. Earth's plates **collide**, or crash into one another. When this happens, the strata are bent, folded, and pushed upward. Over millions of years, the rocks are pushed up into tall **fold mountains**.

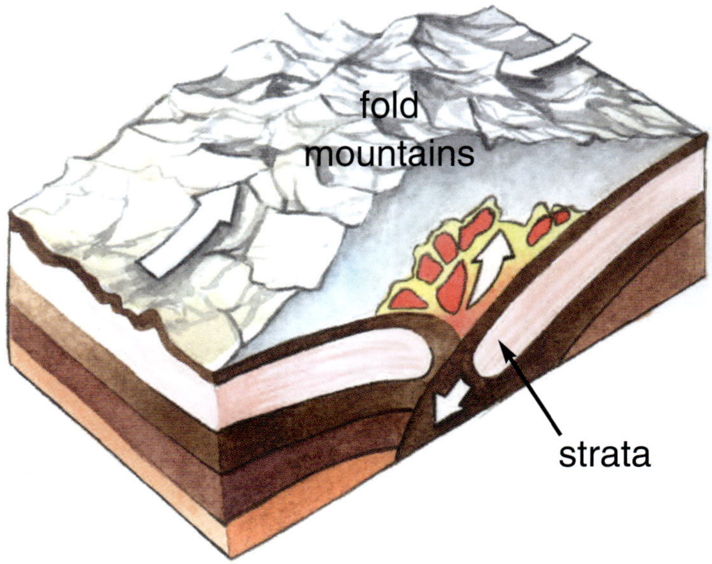

This picture shows how strata are pushed and folded to create mountains.

These fold mountains are part of the Rocky Mountains.

At the edges of continents

Most fold mountains are located at the edges of continents. The edges of continents are where Earth's huge plates collide. The Andes are fold mountains. They run along the west **coast** of South America. A coast is land that is beside an ocean. The Andes make up the longest mountain range in the world, and they are still forming! They grow about four inches (10 cm) every century. A century is 100 years.

Faults and blocks

Earth has many **faults**. Faults are deep cracks in Earth's crust. They are formed when layers of rock are pushed, folded, or twisted too far. Some faults are very long. They stretch for hundreds of miles or kilometers.

These block mountains are part of the Sierra Nevadas in southwestern United States.

Block mountains

When Earth's crust cracks, some of the land along the faults breaks into giant blocks. The blocks are pushed up, down, or sideways by Earth's plates. Over time, the blocks that are pushed upward form big **block mountains**.

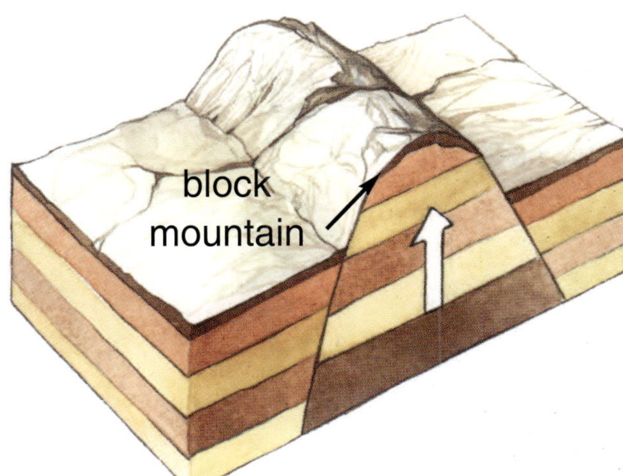

This picture shows how big blocks of rock are pushed upward to form mountains.

Dome mountains

Dome mountains are formed when hot magma rises under the Earth's crust and pushes up the rock above it. Circular mounds called **domes** are formed. The magma cools off and becomes hard rock.

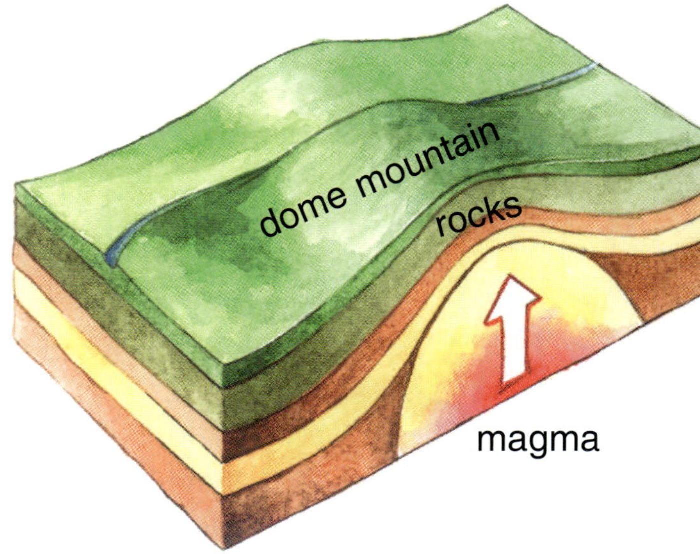

This illustration shows how mountains are formed when magma rises and pushes up rocks.

The Adirondack Mountains in New York State are dome mountains.

Low valleys

Parts of dome mountains slowly wear away. Over time, mountain peaks and **valleys** form. Valleys are low areas of land between mountains. The weather is milder in the valleys than it is in the mountains. Many trees, flowers, and other plants grow there.

This colorful valley is within the Adirondacks. You can see the dome mountains behind it.

Volcanic mountains

Volcanoes are openings in Earth's crust. They can **erupt**, or explode. When volcanoes erupt, hot liquid magma bursts out of them. Magma that bursts out of volcanoes is called lava. Lava flows down the sides of volcanoes. It then cools and turns into hard rock. Volcanic mountains can form on land and in oceans.

This volcano is erupting. Hot lava is pouring out of its ***vent****, or opening.*

Layers of lava

Each time a volcano erupts, lava builds up in hard layers. Over time, the lava may form tall mountains. When a volcano erupts in an ocean, lava spills into the ocean, cools, and becomes hard. After many eruptions, the volcano grows taller. The volcanic mountain rises above the surface of the water. The mountain's top becomes an **island**.

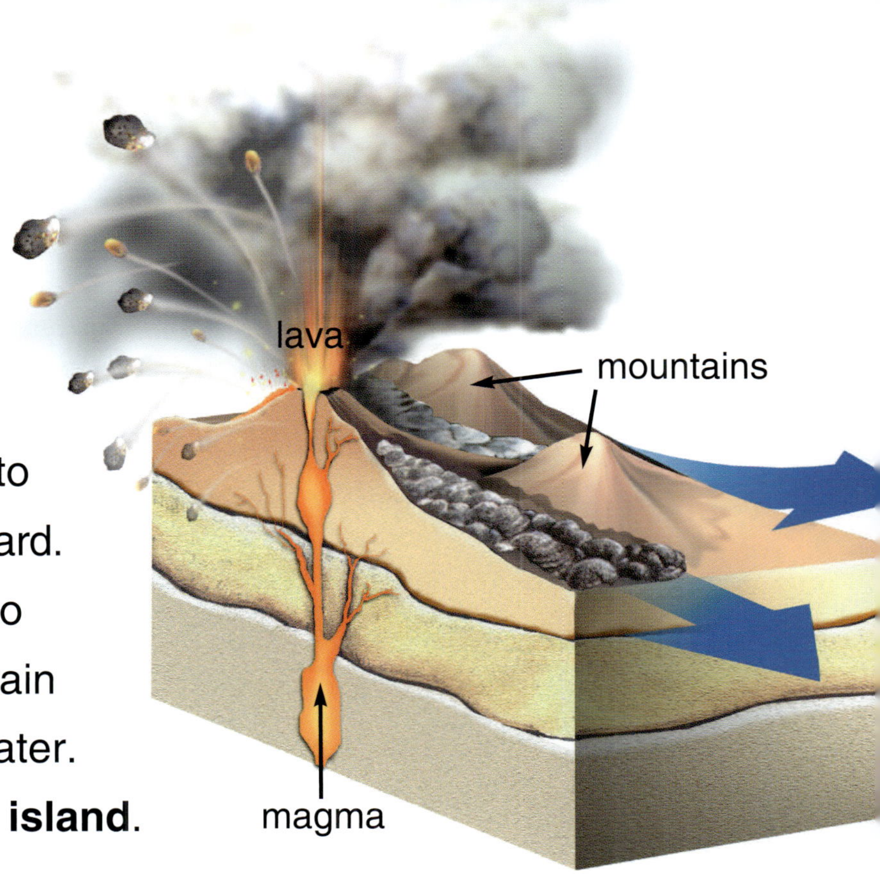

After many years, volcanic mountains in oceans rise above water and become islands. All of the islands in Hawaii are actually the tops of underwater volcanoes.

Changing mountains

Mountains are always changing. They grow bigger over time, but they can also become smaller over time. Mountains become smaller due to **erosion**. Erosion is the natural wearing away of rocks. Rocks are also carried away by wind, rivers, rain, and **glaciers**. Glaciers are huge bodies of ice that move slowly down mountains.

Glaciers pick up large rocks as they move slowly down mountains.

Mountains of trouble

People harm mountains by cutting down trees and other plants that grow on them. Without trees to protect them from wind and water, mountains erode quickly and crumble into pieces of rock. When mountains crumble, dangerous **landslides** can happen. Rocks fall down the sides of mountains and can take homes and cars down with them.

Landslides can happen quickly.

landslide warning sign

People cut down trees on mountains to make room for homes, farms, and roads. They also cut down trees for ***lumber****. Lumber is wood that is used to build homes and other things.*

Mountain plants

Many plants grow on mountains. Different plants grow on different parts of the mountains. The weather at the bottom of a mountain is milder than it is at the top. Fields of flowers and thick **forests** usually grow here. A forest is an area with many trees.

*Flowers grow in colorful **meadows**, or fields, near the bottoms of mountains.*

*Oak, maple, and other **broad-leaved** trees also grow at the bottom of mountains. Broad-leaved trees have flat, wide leaves.*

High on rocky mountains, ***lichens*** *grow. Lichens are plants that are able to grow on rocks.*

Trees stop growing near the top of mountains. The soil is too thin, and the winds are too strong. Strong winds would blow the trees down.

Farther up mountains, ***conifers*** *grow. Conifers are trees with cones and thin leaves that look like needles. Pine and spruce trees are conifers.*

Cold and windy

At the top of very high mountains, the weather is cold, dry, and windy. Trees cannot grow there. The area where trees stop growing is called the **tree line**. Only tough grasses, bushes, and other small plants can survive above the tree line, where there is little soil. The weather is freezing cold and snowy all year long. Very few plants can grow on these cold mountaintops.

Mountain animals

Animals live on mountains on almost every continent. Mountain animals have **adapted**, or become suited, to the harsh environment. Some, such as vicunas and bighorn sheep, have thick coats and **hoofs**. Hoofs help mountain animals climb steep rocks.

Vicunas are relatives of llamas. They live high up on mountains in South America.

Mountain lions are also called cougars. They live in parts of North America and South America. Many mountain lions live in the Rocky Mountains in Canada and the United States.

Living high up

Bighorn sheep also live high up in the Rocky Mountains of North America. They feed on grasses they find. Male bighorns have large curved horns, but the horns of females and their babies are much smaller. Yaks live in the Himalayas. They are among the few animals that can climb such high mountains. People raise yaks for their meat and milk.

People also use yaks to carry heavy loads up very high mountains.

Living on mountains

Many people around the world live on mountains. Some mountain areas are very high up and far from cities. People who live on mountains have learned how to grow food and raise animals to survive. Farmers grow potatoes, rice, and other **crops**. They raise animals such as sheep, goats, llamas, and yaks.

*The Uros people live on a lake high in the Andes mountains. They build their homes and boats from **reeds**. They also use reeds to make the islands on which they live.*

This farmer raises goats for their milk, meat, and wool. He lives in the Himalayas in northern India.

*Farmers often make **terraces**, or steps, on the sides of steep mountains to keep the soil from eroding. They grow crops such as rice and live in villages below the terraces.*

There are cities on mountains, too. People in mountain cities do not have to rely on growing their own food. They can buy food and other things they need in stores.

Mountains of fun!

People visit mountains all over the world. Some people visit mountains to learn more about them. Others visit mountains to hike or climb. Many people love to ski or snowboard down the steep sides of mountains. Most important of all, mountains are beautiful. They make us feel happy to be alive!

Mountains give us a great view of the world below.

These girls met a goat on a mountain.

This boy loves snowboarding down mountains!

One of the most beautiful castles in the world is on top of a mountain in Germany. The castle is called Neuschwanstein. You can climb up the hill to the castle, but it is very tiring!

Words to know

Note: Some boldfaced words are defined where they appear in the book.

continent One of seven large areas of land on Earth

crop A kind of plant grown by people to be used as food or for some other purpose

hoof A hard covering that protects an animal's foot

igneous A type of rock that has formed from magma or lava

island Land that has water all around it

landform A natural feature of land on Earth, such as a mountain

lava Hot liquid magma that flows out of a volcano

magma Hot liquid rock that flows beneath Earth's crust

metamorphic A type of rock that has changed because of heat or pressure

peak The pointed top of a mountain

reed A tall woody grass that grows in water

sedimentary A type of rock that has formed from pieces of soil, sand, or rock that were carried by water, ice, or wind

surface The top layer of something

valley An area of low land between mountains

Index

Adirondacks 18, 19
Alps 9
Andes 8, 9, 15, 28
animals 26-27, 28
base 5
block mountains 17
caves 11
crust 10, 11, 12, 16, 17, 18, 20
dome mountains 18-19
erosion 22, 23, 29
faults 16, 17
fold mountains 14-15
glaciers 22
hills 4, 5
Himalayas 8, 27, 28
landforms 4
landslides 23
lava 11, 20-21
magma 10, 11, 12, 13, 18, 20, 21
mantle 10
Mount Everest 8
Mount Kilimanjaro 7
mountain ranges 8-9, 15
oceans 6, 15, 20, 21
peaks 5, 7, 8, 9, 19
people 23, 27, 28-29, 30
plants 10, 19, 23, 24-25
rocks 4, 10-11, 12, 14, 16, 17, 18, 20, 22, 23, 25, 26
Rocky Mountains 8, 9, 14, 26, 27
sides 4, 5, 20, 23, 29, 30
summits 7
tectonic plates 12-13, 14, 15, 17
valleys 19
volcanoes 11, 20-21